Aspects of the Turf as shown by D

and other French Painter

from Géricault to Bonnard

DEGAS

GERICAULT

LAMI

DE DREUX

BOUDIN

BROWN

PRINCETEAU

FORAIN

ANQUETIN

TOULOUSE-LAUTREC

DUFY

BONNARD

A Loan Exhibition of
Paintings, Drawings and Bronzes

For the Benefit of
The National Museum of Racing, Saratoga

DEGAS'
RACING WORLD

Under the Patronage of the Consul General of
France in New York and Madame Michel Legendre
and The Cultural Counselor to the French Embassy
and Madame Edouard Morot-Sir

MARCH 21ST TO APRIL 27TH

WILDENSTEIN
19 EAST 64TH STREET, NEW YORK

This exhibition has been made possible
through the generosity of the following:

The Walter Art Gallery, Baltimore
Museum of Fine Arts, Boston
The Art Institute of Chicago
The Detroit Institute of Arts
Los Angeles County Museum of Art
The Minneapolis Institute of Arts
Yale University Art Gallery, New Haven, Connecticut
The Metropolitan Museum of Art, New York
The National Gallery of Canada, Ottawa
The Art Museum, Princeton University, Princeton, New Jersey
Museum of Art, Rhode Island School of Design, Providence, R.I.
Shelburne Museum, Vermont
City Art Museum of St. Louis
Santa Barbara Museum of Art
Sterling and Francine Clark Art Institute, Williamstown, Massachusetts

Mr. and Mrs. Walter H. Annenberg
Mr. Walter C. Baker
Mrs. Aldo B. Bertozzi
Mr. and Mrs. Sidney F. Brody
Mr. and Mrs. O. Roy Chalk
Baron de Chollet, Fribourg
Mr. and Mrs. Charles W. Engelhard
Mrs. Anne McDonnell Ford

Mr. and Mrs. David L. Loew

Mr. and Mrs. Paul Mellon

Mr. and Mrs. Hugo Moser

Mr. and Mrs. William S. Paley

Mr. and Mrs. Boris Pregel

Mr. and Mrs. George N. Richard

Mr. Edward Speelman

Mr. Sam Spiegel

Mr. Edgar R. Thom

Mr. and Mrs. John H. Whitney

Mr. and Mrs. Joseph Wohl

and the Anonymous Lenders

INTRODUCTION

Degas' racing world doesn't really exist—at least, not in the conventional sense. He had no marked interest either in the spectacle or the sport. We shall look in vain for a deliberate exploitation of the picturesque and colorful elements inherent in the fashionable gathering; nor, to go to the other extreme, will we find the high-minded message that lies behind Frith's *Derby Day*. Degas had no concern for the race itself. His pictures are valueless for the racetrack historian. He never produced an equestrian portrait (which even Corot, Courbet, Manet and Renoir all did); he never added to the stock of portraits of famous race horses; and he never troubled to record a specific race. Two of his paintings are vaguely connected with Epsom; four others have settings at Longchamp. But none of them provides the least indication of a particular meeting, nor could owners' colors be identified. Yet all this said, the world of racing occupied Degas' attention, intermittently it is true, from 1860 until 1900. Some 45 paintings, 20 pastels, 250 drawings and 17 sculptures bear witness to his tireless curiosity.

Unlike Géricault, De Dreux and the young Toulouse-Lautrec, Degas was not a brilliant horseman—indeed, it seems extremely doubtful that he ever rode at all. This non-involvement partly explains his withdrawn attitude towards the horse. No Romantic steeds, images of uncontrolled energy, appear in his work. Even when he depicts, in an early history-picture, Alexander subduing the wild horse Bucephalus he is markedly prosaic, giving nothing of the fiery combat that a Géricault or a Delacroix would have emphasized. He saw his task as the subduing of the horse—artistically; the challenge of its form and movements had to be met with a calm, controlling hand. Only rarely, and then for contrast, did he introduce an excited, *mouvementé* horse in his compositions. Yet for all their apparent anonymity, Degas' horse pictures are not self-contained creations: they do owe something to an earlier tradition and make use of specific contemporary discoveries.

In the fall of 1861, at the age of 27, Degas visited Ménil-Hubert, near Ornes, the Normandy estates of his school-friend, Henri Valpinçon. It was his first real experience of the Normandy landscape and he recorded his impressions at length in one of his notebooks. He thought the countryside was "exactly like England, large and small fields enclosed by hedges, humid paths, ponds—green and umber." He found a more precise analogy when he looked down from the terrace behind the château: the view, he wrote, was "absolutely similar to that in those colored English prints of hunting and racing scenes." It was no coincidence that Degas should see this landscape through the remembered image of the English sporting-print (he was also reading Fielding's *Tom Jones* at the time and had made copies of some of Hogarth's engravings, but by 1861 he had not yet visited England). His remarks, as we shall see, reflect a strong contemporary admiration for the English sporting-print. But their implications for Degas himself are best seen in two small paintings which date from 1871.

The first, *Carriage at the Races* (now in the Museum of Fine Arts, Boston), shows a delicate balance between portrait, landscape and genre. In the foreground, seated in a victoria, are Henri Valpinçon and his family, united by admiring glance and gesture for the baby in the nurse's lap. An open, light-filled landscape extends behind them, peopled by figures on horseback and a gentleman in a gig; the object of their interest is a race-meeting. Three galloping horses may be seen, their front and hind legs at full stretch in the conventional pose of the sporting-print. It is as if Degas has brought together in one picture the experience of his visit to Normandy a decade earlier: he pays homage to his host, to the landscape and to the English sporting-print.

DEGAS, Carriage at the Races *Museum of Fine Arts, Boston*

The second painting is strikingly different in mood and content. The scene is an interior, an office, one presumes, with a man seated, arms folded, at a desk scattered with papers, while a young woman leans over the back of a chair. It is a closed, intimate and enigmatic painting; glances now become scowls and pouts; there is an uneasy undertone of conflict, which has provoked much discussion on the title and interpretation of the content. It is now generally known as *Bouderie* or *Sulking*. [No. 6] But in all this debate, one prominent part of the picture has tended to get overlooked. On the wall behind the two sitters hangs a framed painting depicting a steeplechase. It is in fact a precise copy of a sporting-print by J. F. Herring (1795-1865), entitled *Steeplechase Cracks*.

Degas was by no means alone in his admiration for the relatively minor art form of the sporting-print. Even his assumption that it provided an accurate representation of the English landscape finds an echo in Théophile Gautier's comments on his visit to Ascot in June 1849: "One saw the living reality of the English sporting-prints and cherry-colored horses, emerald fields and jonquil carriages which, in Ritner and Goupil's window, cast doubts upon English art. A visit to Ascot justifies them completely." Many cultivated Parisians formed their idea of England from this source. Prints were in plentiful supply at such dealers as Ritner and Goupil (and even today, one can easily pick up copies on the Paris quais). For French painters, the interest went back to Carle Vernet, Géricault and the youthful Delacroix. And the older Delacroix could still enthuse over the prints of Alken, some of which he actually copied. A note in his Journal for March 26, 1863 reads: "Carrier, who came to call on me, has promised me some Alken prints."

The vogue for the sporting-print was but one aspect of a general admiration for things English, which included Constable's painting, Shakespeare, Byron and Scott — and pantomime (one of Baudelaire's enthusiasms). But it also coincided with the rapid spread of horse racing in France under Louis-Philippe and Napoleon III. For racing in France on any scale was a fundamentally nineteenth century phenomenon. The first English Derby was run in 1780, its French equivalent not until 1836. The English Jockey Club was founded in 1750, its French counterpart in 1833. The racetrack at Longchamp wasn't opened until 1857; and it was only in 1863 that the *Société des Steeplechases de France* was founded.

This growing interest demanded interpretation from artists. Many minor and now forgotten figures moved in, continuing, often in prints, the traditions established by English sporting artists. They would record the various stages of a race— the Weighing-in, the Saddling, the Start and the Finish, and, of course, the moment when the race was in full flight. Accurate reportage was the major requirement, leaving little room for artistic invention. Only one artist had been able to infuse new meaning into the tame conventions of the sporting-print. Géricault's *Derby at Epsom* of 1821 raises a piece of genre to the level of a grand, monumental statement. And his other pictures of horse races have more the quality of antique reliefs than contemporary reportage.

In the forty years between Géricault's *Derby at Epsom* and Degas' first visit to Normandy, a fashionable clientèle desired a fashionable picture. Alfred de Dreux (1810-60) supplied the need. A keen horseman, like Géricault, a great admirer of the English thoroughbred, and a frequent visitor to England, he gave an immediately pleasing evocation of the hunt and the racetrack. A loose and facile technique ("bright and dazzling...having the fresh and vivid appearance of theatrical decors" was how Baudelaire described his work in 1845) enabled him to capture the superficial glamour and glitter and assured his modish acceptability. Eugène Lami (1800-90) brought a similar facility and an illustrator's eye to the task. Their descendants are John-Lewis Brown and René Princeteau.

Manet's fleeting infatuation with the racetrack promised to re-invigorate the tradition. Certainly, in his *Races at Longchamp* of 1864 (Art Institute of Chicago) he conveys the speed and excitement by the novel device, possibly inspired by photography, of adopting a head-on view of the horses as they rush down the track. But this remained an isolated instance. Another Manet racetrack painting (Mr. J. H. Whitney collection), was commissioned by a racing enthusiast, a certain Monsieur Barret, in 1872. Here he simply resorts to the traditional profile representation of galloping horses as seen in sporting-prints. Indeed, he confessed to Berthe Morisot: "Not being in the habit of painting horses, I copied mine from those who know best how to do them."

One of the strangest omissions in the whole of French nineteenth century painting is the complete lack of interest among the Impressionist painters in the racetrack as a potential subject. Even Boudin could occasionally use the excuse of the races at Deauville for a perceptive rendering of the effects of outdoor light. And

Degas himself had pointed the way in the luminously enveloped landscape of his *Carriage at the Races,* which was exhibited at the first Impressionist exhibition of 1874. Monet and Renoir in particular would surely have delighted in the subtle play of sunlight on horse and turf; or would have caught the contrasting patches of color in the enclosure. Here was a subject made for them. But it was not to be. Only two of their descendants took it up; Bonnard, fitfully, in the 1890's, reducing the scene to his customary series of simplified shapes and flat patterns. And, later, of course, Dufy swiftly caught, in a post-Fauvist idiom, the atmosphere of Ascot and Epsom.

It was thus left to Degas to interpret the rapidly expanding interest in horse-racing. Or rather, to use this 'modernity' as a cloak in which to wrap his essential concern: the horse. This could take several forms. Consider the painting which he sent to the Paris Salon of 1866, *Scène de Steeple-Chase: Aux courses, le jockey blessé.* It was a subject dear to the English sporting artist; a scene from a steeple-chase, showing a jump where a jockey had been thrown. Many prints by Alken and others were devoted to the theme, often giving it an amusing twist, emphasizing the sense of the ridiculous in the fallen horse and the tumbled rider. But it could be treated more seriously, as may be seen in the J. F. Herring print that Degas included in the background of *Bouderie.* And it was with the highest seriousness that he chose to represent the subject. In preparing it, he made a considerable number of drawings—some twenty have survived. From those in the Clark Art Institute [Nos. 24 and 25] and the collection of Baron de Chollet, [Nos. 26-29] we can see how Degas played with alternative possibilities. These, however, were not based on his own observation; they were largely derived from English sporting-prints. The only 'original' drawings were those of his brother Achille who posed for the figure of the wounded jockey. The small, unfinished painting from the collection of Mr. Sam Spiegel [No. 3] shows one solution. The Salon picture, measuring six by five feet, and now in the collection of Mr. and Mrs. Paul Mellon, shows a more ambitious treatment of his sources. Here, Degas has presented a close-up image, in which the diagonal downward movement of the horses dominates the picture space. The landscape is just summarily indicated. His attitude toward the subject is peculiarly laconic and non-involved; there is no attempt to heighten the dramatic content. (The deadpan element is even more striking in another version, now in Basle). Degas, then, has taken a slice of modern life, added more than a dash of the sporting-print, and then endeavoured to give them the status of history-painting.

A more direct pointer to his future work may be found in his two earliest paintings of the racetrack, the so-called *Jockeys at Epsom* [No. 1] and *At the Races,* now in the Fogg Art Museum. The idea sprang from a notebook jotting of 1860, where Degas speaks of doing a composition of two racehorses with two jockeys, the terrain green like a cut lawn and behind a quiet village in the hills. It is noteworthy that in this same year, he had made several pencil copies from Gozzoli's *Procession of the Magi* in the Palazzo Riccardi in Florence, a composition which contains, more ornately embellished, similar elements to his proposed racetrack picture. Following his notebook jotting, Degas then made several preparatory drawings for the horses; and ultimately, a compositional study (Clark Art Institute) [No. 22] which served for the version now in the Fogg. The choice of the moment before the start, the predominantly profile arrangement of the horses and their near-parallel disposition in the picture space, combine to give a processional air to the painting. And the movements of the horses have a rather deliberate stiff-

DEGAS, Scène de Steeple-Chase, Aux courses, le jockey blessé
Mr. and Mrs. Paul Mellon Collection

ness, which again reminds one of Gozzoli. Nonetheless, this was a composition that Degas returned to later, in a painting now in the Louvre and in a group of pastels executed in 1882.

In the 1860's Degas began observing horses for himself, which he could do quite easily during his stays with Henri Valpinçon, whose estate lay close to Haras-le-Pin, one of the foremost horse-breeding establishments in France. Many pencil studies exist, showing how he explored the form of the horse from every conceivable angle. The majority were done quickly, with an exploratory but decisive line; a few were given a more elaborate finish, as in the saddled horse from the Bertozzí collection [No. 33]. But he also concentrated his attentions on the jockeys, relentlessly analysing their bodily tensions in the saddle. The brush drawings from the

Chicago Art Institute [No. 23] and the collection of Walter C. Baker [No. 30] show a remarkably assured handling, crisply noting the form and subtly simulating the silks. Another element is introduced in a group of pencil drawings, to which that in the W. S. Paley collection belongs [No. 38]. Degas not only watches a hand loosely holding a rein, or describes a foot slipped through the stirrup, its weight clearly felt, or notes the shadow cast by a cap; he also conveys something of the jockey's physiognomy. This portrait-quality, and also the style of the drawing, are reminiscent of such studies of female sitters as *Mme. Hertel* and *Mme. Gaujelin*. Indeed, it suggests that he sometimes used friends rather than anonymous professional jockeys as models (later, in 1882, he was to use his artist-friend, Baron Lepic, in such a way) [No. 49]. In the late 1860's, and early seventies, however, he did make portrait-studies of his brother, Achille [32], and of Manet [31]—but as spectators, not jockeys.

All these drawings formed a readily available pattern-book which Degas consulted for a group of paintings executed between 1868 and 1872. And just as his early theatre and dance pictures have identifiable settings—the stage and rehearsal rooms of the Opera—so several of these race-track compositions provide glimpses of Longchamp. In the *Racehorses* [No. 5] the horses are seen walking towards the start, with Mont Valerien in the background. In the *False Start* [No. 4] Degas introduces the recently erected stand and enclosure. This is based on a carefully notated pencil drawing, also in the collection of Mr. J. H. Whitney. But Degas' scrupulous observation, his unerring sense of composition, and his use of clear, vivid color accents raise the paintings above the merely topographical.

Degas' enthusiasm for the horse tended to diminish in the late 1870's. New themes occupied him—dancers, laundresses and café-concert singers. He exhibited three of his racetrack pictures in London in 1872 and at the first Impressionist exhibition two years later, he included the *False Start*, as well as *Carriage at the Races*. But only one other was shown at a later Impressionist exhibition—that of 1879. In the 1870's therefore, he could by no means have had a widespread reputation as a painter of horses. The only commission he undertook was a repetition of one of his compositions for J. B. Faure, the opera singer and great collector of Manet and the Impressionists.

His interest revived in 1882. He made new drawings, now using charcoal, chalk and sometimes blue crayon to create bold and summary effects. His paintings of the 1880's show similar abbreviations. Landscape backgrounds grow increasingly more generalized, spectators are either eliminated or, at most, become a series of arbitrary marks in the distance. Generally we are alone with the horses and jockeys: *we* become the spectators, observing their ritual. Degas continued to use a relatively small format; one difference from his earlier work was the frequent use of panel as a support. Two of these are included in the present exhibition (Clark Art Institute, Williamstown, and Walters Art Gallery, Baltimore) [Nos. 10 and 11], where one can compare Degas' ingenious variations on a given motif; and contrast the sensuous quality of the paint in the one with the thin, stained effect—the wood graining showing through—in the other.

Degas' continuing ability to enlarge his stock of poses may be seen in the frieze-like composition from the Paul Mellon collection [No. 7]. The seemingly casual disposition of the horses and their apparently spontaneous movement have nonetheless been artfully contrived. The pose of the central rearing animal is taken up by the adjoining one, seen in profile, and echoed again in the one further behind. This is an art of calculated interval, eloquent phrasing and meaningful contrasts. And the same applies to the startling close-up in the small oil from the Yale University Art Gallery [No. 9], an affair of segments and slices compressed in space. Thus did Degas commit his acts of premeditated instantaneity.

His series of pastels, begun in the 1880's, cast a similar spell. One of the finest is that dating from c. 1884, now in the collection of Mr. Charles W. Engelhard, [No. 14] which provides a subtle variation on the Boston painting of more than a decade earlier. The pastel from the collection of Mr. Walter Annenberg, [No. 13] which once belonged to the French critic, Theodore Duret, also reinterprets a composition first used in two oils of the 1870's. It is however, unique among Degas' pastels in being executed on panel. Those like the No. 12, and the No. 16 in the Brody Collection, show a vibrant use of the medium, in which the hatchings and superimposed layers enrich the surface. And from the racetrack, Degas can take us to the early morning training, in a pastel that has a piquantly asymmetrical lay-out.

Degas' obsession with the horse found a further outlet in sculpture. As early as 1868, he had modelled a horse in wax. This was evidently used as an aid to the painting of the horse in his Salon picture *Mlle. Fiocre dans le Ballet "La Source"*. But it was only in the 1880's that he returned to it. Some of these sculptures were clearly based on his own drawings: compare the sheet from Santa Barbara [No. 40], which is in fact two studies of the same horse seen from different angles, with the sculpture of the *Horse Standing* (Rewald III). But another source was the series of photographs of horses which the American photographer E. J. Muybridge, published in his book *Animal Locomotion* (1887). These demolished many cherished conventions concerning the movement of the horse; in particular, they showed that a galloping horse never at any stage had both front and hind legs extended. Several of Degas' sculptures which depict trotting and galloping horses were clearly derived from Muybridge. It is as if he suddenly wished to render those movements which he had virtually ignored in his paintings and pastels. All his sculptures were modelled in wax and only cast in bronze after his death.

But the final word must rest with a pastel (National Gallery of Canada, Ottawa) [No. 17]. Appropriately, for it was the last work that Degas devoted to the racehorse (it must date from the late 1890's). The presentation is of the simplest: four horses overlap in a series of contrasting axes and the setting is reduced to three horizontal bands. It hardly matters that Degas has skilfully disguised the fact that two of the horses are based on Muybridge. With fierce, expressive, abrupt strokes of pastel, he has created a compelling image and a monumental presence. To put a De Dreux, a Princeteau or a John-Lewis Brown against this is to put a piece of first-rate journalism, let us say, against Flaubert's *Sentimental Education*, or to compare the finest fashion-plate with a Cézanne portrait. The distance is surely so great between an artist who creates for posterity and one who titillates the tastes of the moment.

RONALD PICKVANCE
LECTURER IN FINE ART
UNIVERSITY OF NOTTINGHAM

CATALOGUE

DEGAS
1834-1917
OILS and PASTELS

1. Jockeys at Epsom, 1860-62
   Oil, 11½ x 9 inches   L. 75*
   Lent Anonymously

2. The Morning Ride, 1864-68
    Oil, 31⅞ x 25½ inches   L. 118
    Lent by The Detroit Institute of Arts

3. At the Races, the Wounded Jockey, c. 1866
   Oil, 10¾ x 16½ inches   L. 142
   Lent by Mr. Sam Spiegel

4. The False Start, 1869-72

   Oil, 12½ x 15¾ inches   L. 258

   From the Collection of Mr. and Mrs. John Hay Whitney

5. Race Horses at Longchamp, 1873-75
   Oil, 11¾ x 15¾ inches L. 334
   Lent by The Museum of Fine Arts, Boston (S. A. Denio Collection)

6. Sulking, 1873-75
  Oil, 12½ x 18⅛ inches L. 335
  Lent by The Metropolitan Museum of Art (The H. O. Havemeyer Collection)

At the Races, Before the Start, 1878-80

Oil, 15¾ x 35 inches   L. 502

Lent by Mr. and Mrs. Paul Mellon

8. The Trainers, c. 1880
   Pastel, 15¼ x 35¾ inches   L. 597 bis
   Lent by Mr. and Mrs. Joseph Wohl

9. The Jockeys, 1881-85

Oil, 10¼ x 15⅜ inches   L. 680

Lent by The Yale University Art Gallery, New Haven

10. Before the Race, c. 1882
   Oil on panel, 10¾ x 14⅛ inches   L. 702
   Lent by The Sterling and Francine Clark Art Institute, Williamstown

11. Before the Race, c. 1882
    Oil on panel, 10⅜ x 13¾ inches
    Lent by The Walters Art Gallery, Baltimore

12. Three Jockeys, 1883-90
   Pastel, 19¼ x 24½ inches   L. 763
   Lent Anonymously

13. Race Horses, c. 1885
    Pastel on panel, 12½ x 15⅞ inches   L. 852
    Lent by Mr. and Mrs. Walter H. Annenberg

14. Before the Start, c. 1886
   Pastel, 19¾ x 25 inches   L. 878
   Lent by Mr. and Mrs. Charles W. Engelhard

15. The Jockeys, 1886-90
    Oil, 10¼ x 14 inches   L. 896 bis
    Lent by Mr. Edgar R. Thom

16. Before the Start, c. 1893
    Pastel, 25½ x 28¾ inches   L. 1143
    Lent by Mr. and Mrs. Sidney F. Brody

17. Race Horses   Late Nineties
   Pastel, 21¼ x 24¾ inches   L. 756
   Lent by The National Gallery of Canada, Ottawa

DEGAS
DRAWINGS

18. At the Races, 1862
    Pencil, 13¾ x 19 inches
    V. IV, 253
    Lent by The Sterling and Francine Clark Art Institute, Williamstown

*"V" refers to "Vente", *Catalogue des Tableaux, Pastels et Dessins par Edgar Degas et provenant de son Atelier, *Paris 1918 & 1919

19. Horse, 1860-65
  Pencil, 12⅝ x 9⅞ inches
  V. IV, 201 (b)
  Lent by The Museum of Art, Rhode Island School of Design, Providence

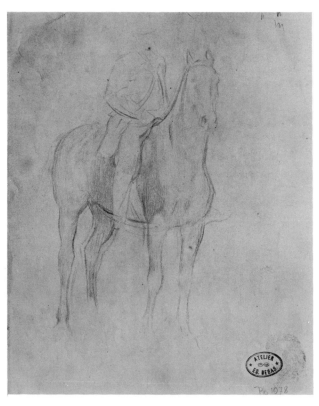

20. Rider Looking to the Right, 1860-65
  Pencil, 5¼ x 8¼ inches
  Lent by Baron de Chollet, Fribourg

21. Jockey on Horseback in Profile, 1860-65
    Pencil, 8⅛ x 10½ inches
    Lent by Baron de Chollet, Fribourg

22. Plough Horse, 1860-61
    Pencil, 5¾ x 7⅞ inches
    Lent by Baron de Chollet, Fribourg

23. Four Studies of a Jockey, c. 1866
   Brush with oil, 17¼ x 11¾ inches
   V. III, 114 (1)
   Lent by The Art Institute of Chicago
   (Mr. and Mrs. Lewis L. Coburn Memorial Collection)

24. Study for "The Wounded Jockey", c. 1866
   Charcoal, 9⅜ x 14 inches
   V. IV, 241 (a)
   Lent by The Sterling and Francine Clark Art Institute, Williamstown

25. Study for "The Wounded Jockey", c. 1866
Black Chalk heightened with white, 12⅜ x 17⅝ inches
V. IV, 241 (b)
Lent by The Sterling and Francine Clark Art Institute, Williamstown

26. The Wounded Jockey, c. 1866
Charcoal, 9 x 12¼ inches
V. III, 353 (b)
Lent by Baron de Chollet, Fribourg

27. The Wounded Jockey and Studies of Horses, c. 1866
Pencil and Charcoal, 13½ x 8¾ inches
V. IV, 232 (b)
Lent by Baron de Chollet, Fribourg

28. Horses Galloping, c. 1866
Pencil, 5½ x 8 inches
Lent by Baron de Chollet, Fribourg

29. The Fall, c. 1866
   Pencil, 5½ x 8½ inches
   Lent by Baron de Chollet, Fribourg

30. Jockey on Horseback, 1870-72
   Black chalk, brush and gouache, 11⅜ x 6¾ inches
   V. III, 128 (2)
   Lent by Mr. Walter C. Baker

31. Edouard Manet at the Races, c. 1870
Graphite Pencil, 12¾ x 9¾ inches
V. II, 210 (3)
*Lent by The Metropolitan Museum
of Art (Rogers Fund, 1918)*

32. Achille Degas, 1872-73
Oil on Paper, 14½ x 9¼ inches L. 307
Lent by The Minneapolis Institute of Arts

33. Saddled Horse, c. 1873
   Pencil, 9 x 11¾ inches
   V. IV, 209 (b)
   Lent by Mrs. Aldo B. Bertozzi

34. Jockey on Horseback, 1874
   Charcoal with pastel, 7⅛ x 4 5/16 inches
   Lent by a Private Collector, Paris

35. Horse Seen in Profile, and Jockey, c. 1875
    Pencil, 7½ x 10½ inches
    Lent by Baron de Chollet, Fribourg

36. The Rider, 1875-77
    Brush and black ink, 9⅝ x 13½ inches, L. 383 bis
    Lent by The Sterling and Francine Clark Art Institute, Williamstown

37. Jockey, 1878
     Pencil, 11⅜ x 9 inches
     Study for L. 387 or L. 461, V. III, 128 (1)
     Lent by The Detroit Institute of Arts

38. Jockey, 1878
     Pencil, 9 x 12¾ inches
     V. IV, 260 (a)
     Lent by Mr. and Mrs. William S. Paley

39. Jockey, c. 1878
   Pencil, 13¾ x 8¼ inches
   V. III, 92 (1)
   Lent by Baron de Chollet, Fribourg

40. Two Horses, 1880
   Charcoal, 8½ x 12 inches
   V. IV, 200
   Lent by The Santa Barbara Museum of Art

. Two Horses, 1881-85
9½ x 12 inches
Lent by Baron de Chollet, Fribourg

42. The Rider, 1881-85
   Charcoal, 12¼ x 9 inches
   V. III, 96 (2)
   Lent by Baron de Chollet, Fribourg

43. Jockey, 1881-85
   Charcoal, 13¾ x 8½ inches
   V. III, 90 (1)
   Lent by Mrs. Aldo B. Bertozzi

44. Three Studies of Jockeys, 1881-85
   Charcoal, 4¾ x 3 inches each
   Lent by Baron de Chollet, Fribourg

45. Rider on a Galloping Horse, 1881-85
Charcoal, 11¼ x 7¼ inches
Lent by Baron de Chollet, Fribourg

46. Jockey and Horse in Profile, 1881-85
Black Crayon, 10 x 15 inches
Lent by Baron de Chollet, Fribourg

47. Rider and Amazon, 1881-85
9⅞ x 7½ inches
Lent by Baron de Chollet, Fribourg

48. Amazon, 1881-85
Charcoal, 10½ x 7¼ inches
Lent by Baron de Chollet, Fribourg

49. Portrait of Baron Lepic, 1882
   Pencil, 12 x 9 inches
   V. IV, 215 (a)
   Lent by Mr. and Mrs. David L. Loew

dy of a Jockey, c. 1882

arcoal with pastel, 19 x 25 inches

II, 355

t by Mr. and Mrs. Boris Pregel

51. Two Jockeys, 1882-84
    Charcoal and blue crayon, 9¼ x 12⅝ inches
    V. III, 353
    Lent by The Museum of Art, Rhode Island School of Design, Providence

52. Jockey, 1882-84
    Charcoal, 13¾ x 8½ inches
    V. III, 108
    Lent by Baron de Chollet, Fribourg

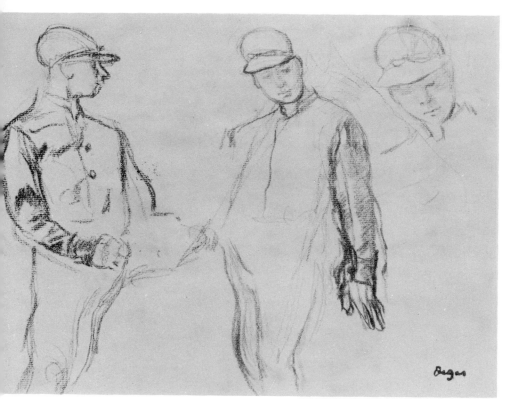

Three Studies of a Jockey, 1882-84
Black and blue pencil, 9 x 11¾ inches
. III, 104 (b), Study for L. 755
ent by Baron de Chollet, Fribourg

54. Race Horses, 1882-84
    Charcoal, 9½ x 12½ inches
    V. IV, 383 (b)
    Lent by Baron de Chollet, Fribourg

55. Jockey on Horseback, 1882-84
     Charcoal with pastel, 11¾ x 9 inches
     V. III, 109 (3)
     Lent by Baron de Chollet, Fribourg

56. Study of Jockeys, c. 1885
     Charcoal, 24 x 12 inches
     V. III, 377
     Lent by The Art Museum, Princeton University

57. Jockey, 1885-90
   Black crayon with pastel, 12⅝ x 9½ inches
   V. IV, 231 (b)
   Lent by Baron de Chollet, Fribourg

58. Jockey Seen from Back, c. 1889
   Charcoal, 10½ x 13¾ inches
   Study for L. 986
   Lent by Baron de Chollet, Fribourg

59. Rider Looking to the Left, 1890
    11½ x 8⅞ inches
    Lent by Baron de Chollet, Fribourg

60. Jockey on Horseback, c. 1890
    10¼ x 7½ inches
    V. III, 106 (3)
    Lent by Baron de Chollet, Fribourg

61. Jockey
   Pencil, 12¼ x 8¼ inches
   V. III, 93 (3)
   Lent by Baron de Chollet, Fribourg

62. Jockey
   Pencil, 13 x 9 inches
   V. III, 107 (1)
   Lent by Baron de Chollet, Fribourg

63. Jockey on Horseback
Pencil, 7⅞ x 4¾ inches
Lent by Baron de Chollet, Fribourg

64. Rider Turning Backwards
Pencil and watercolor, 6¾ x 8¾ inches
Lent by Baron de Chollet, Fribourg

65. Jockey and Two Studies of Horses
   Pencil, 12 x 9¼ inches
   Lent by Baron de Chollet, Fribourg

66. Jockey on a Stopped Horse
   Pencil, 4½ x 5 inches
   Lent by Baron de Chollet, Fribourg

67. Jockey on Horseback
   Pencil, 11 x 8¾ inches
   Lent by Baron de Chollet, Fribourg

68. Walking Horse
   Pencil and ink, 8¾ x 11⅝ inches
   Lent by Baron de Chollet, Fribourg

69. Studies of Draught Horses
   Pencil, 7⅞ x 13 inches
   Lent by Baron de Chollet, Fribourg

70. Head of a Horse
   Pencil, 4½ x 3¼ inches
   Lent by Baron de Chollet, Fribourg

71. Horse with Lowered Head, Rear View
Pencil, 5⅝ x 5⅝ inches
Lent by Baron de Chollet, Fribourg

72. Head of a Trainer
Pencil, 4½ x 3 inches
Lent by Baron de Chollet, Fribourg

THEODORE GERICAULT (1791-1824)

EUGENE-LOUIS LAMI (1800-1890)

ALFRED DE DREUX (1810-1860)

EUGENE BOUDIN (1824-1898)

JOHN LEWIS BROWN (1829-1890)

RENE PRINCETEAU (1843-1914)

JEAN-LOUIS FORAIN (1852-1931)

LOUIS ANQUETIN (1861-1932)

HENRI DE TOULOUSE-LAUTREC (1864-1901)

PIERRE BONNARD (1867-1947)

RAOUL DUFY (1877-1955)

GERICAULT

73. Jockey on a Race Horse
Oil, 14½ x 18¼ inches
Lent by Mr. and Mrs. Paul Mellon

LAMI

74. At the Races
Watercolor, 6⅝ x 13⅜ inches
Lent by Mr. and Mrs. Paul Mellon

DE DREUX

75. Jockey on Horseback
   Oil, 23¼ x 28¾ inches
   Lent by Mr. and Mrs. Paul Mellon

DE DREUX

76. Jockey on Horseback Led by a Lad
   Oil, 23¼ x 28¾ inches
   Lent by Mr. and Mrs. Paul Mellon

DE DREUX

77. Steeplechase
   Oil, 17 x 25¾ inches
   Lent by Mr. Edward Speelman

DE DREUX

78. The Thoroughbred
   Watercolor, 8 x 11¾ inches
   Lent by Mr. and Mrs. Paul Mellon

DE DREUX

79. Three Jockeys Training
Gouache and Watercolor, 5½ x 8 inches
Lent by Baron de Chollet, Fribourg

DE DREUX

80. Trainer and Two Horses
Gouache and Watercolor, 6¾ x 10 inches
Lent by Baron de Chollet, Fribourg

BOUDIN

81. Races at Deauville, 1866

Oil, 15 13/16 x 25⅝ inches

Lent by Mrs. Anne McDonnell Ford

BOUDIN

82. Races at Deauville, 1866
   Watercolor, 8 x 12¼ inches
   Lent by Mr. and Mrs. Paul Mellon

BROWN

83. Steeplechase
   Oil, 13⅜ x 10¼ inches
   Lent by a Private Collector, New York

BROWN

84. At the Races

Oil, 24¾ x 25¼ inches

Lent by a Private Collector, New York

PRINCETEAU

85. Jockey Training
   Oil, 22⅞ x 28½ inches
   Lent Anonymously

PRINCETEAU

86. Three Jockeys Training, Oil
   Lent by a Private Collector, London

PRINCETEAU

87. Racing Scene
Drawing, 11½ x 16¾ inches
Lent by Mr. Edward Speelman

PRINCETEAU

88. Racing Scene
Drawing, 8½ x 11 inches
Lent by Mr. Edward Speelman

PRINCETEAU

89. Race Horses
    Pencil, 7 9/16 x 11 inches
    Lent Anonymously

FORAIN

90. Races at Deauville
    Watercolor, 18 x 23¾ inches
    Lent by Mr. and Mrs. Paul Mellon

FORAIN

91. Races at Longchamp
Oil, 29 x 36½ inches
Lent by Mr. and Mrs. Paul Mellon

FORAIN

92. "Le Bon Tuyau" ("The Good Tip")
Oil, 10⅝ x 13⅞ inches
Lent by Mr. and Mrs. Paul Mellon

FORAIN

93. At the Races
Oil, 10½ x 14¾ inches
Lent by a Private Collector, London

ANQUETIN

94. The Finish of the Grand Prix at Longchamp, c. 1893
   Oil, 19¾ x 28¾ inches
   Lent by Mr. Edward Speelman

ANQUETIN

95. At the Races
   Watercolor, 13⅜ x 17 inches
   Lent by a Private Collector, New York

TOULOUSE-LAUTREC

96. At the Races, "La Loge", 1888-89
Oil, 15 x 11 inches
Lent by Mr. and Mrs. O. Roy Chalk

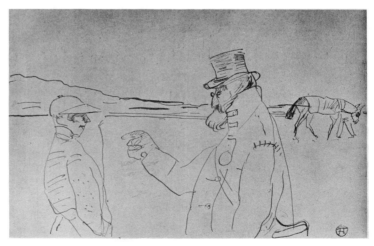

TOULOUSE-LAUTREC

97. Jockey and Owner, c. 1895
Pen, 9 x 13⅞ inches
Lent by The Los Angeles County Museum of Art

TOULOUSE-LAUTREC

98. Jockey on Horseback, 1884
Ink, 7¼ x 5 inches
Lent by Mr. and Mrs. Hugo Moser

TOULOUSE-LAUTREC

99. Amazon
Ink, 4⅜ x 3⅜ inches
Lent by Baron de Chollet, Fribourg

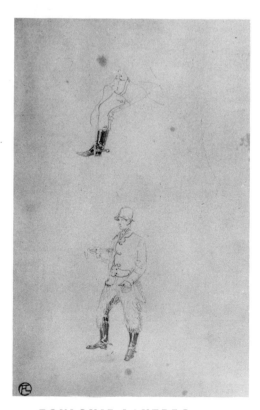

TOULOUSE-LAUTREC

100. Jockey
Pencil, 13½ x 8¼ inches
Lent by Baron de Chollet, Fribourg

TOULOUSE-LAUTREC

101. Jockey on a Rearing Horse
Ink, 3⅝ x 5¾ inches
Lent by Baron de Chollet, Fribourg

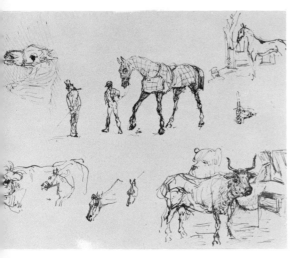

TOULOUSE-LAUTREC

Horses and Cows

Ink, 6-7/16 x 8⅛ inches

Lent by Baron de Chollet, Fribourg

TOULOUSE-LAUTREC

103. Jockey

Pencil, 6-5/16 x 7½ inches

Lent by Baron de Chollet, Fribourg

TOULOUSE-LAUTREC

104. The Cart

Pencil, 5¾ x 8¾ inches

Lent by Baron de Chollet, Fribourg

TOULOUSE-LAUTREC

105. The Rider

Ink, 5¾ x 7-3/16 inches

Lent by Baron de Chollet, Fribourg

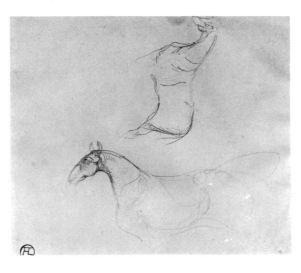

TOULOUSE-LAUTREC

106. Two Horses

Pencil, 7½ x 9 inches

Lent by Baron de Chollet, Fribourg

BONNARD

107. "Sous Les Ordres"
Oil, 13 x 19⅛ inches
Lent by Mr. and Mrs. Paul Mellon

BONNARD

108. At the Races, 1894
    Watercolor, 7½ x 7¼ inches
    Lent by Mr. and Mrs. Paul Mellon

BONNARD

The Start

Oil, 11⅝ x 16⅞ inches

Lent Anonymously

DUFY

110. The Grandstand at Ascot, 1935
Watercolor, 19½ x 24⅞ inches
Lent by Mr. and Mrs. Paul Mellon

DUFY

111. Races at Epsom, 1938
Watercolor, 19¼ x 24⅜ inches
Lent by Mr. and Mrs. Paul Mellon

DEGAS
BRONZES

112. Horse at Trough
    Height: 6⅜ inches R. II*
    Lent by Mr. and Mrs. George N. Richard

"R" stands for John Rewald, Degas, Sculpture, New York, 1956

113. Horse Walking   Cire Perdue A.A. Hebrard $\frac{11}{A}$
Height: 8⅞ inches R. IV
Lent by The Metropolitan Museum of Art (The H. O. Havemeyer Collection)

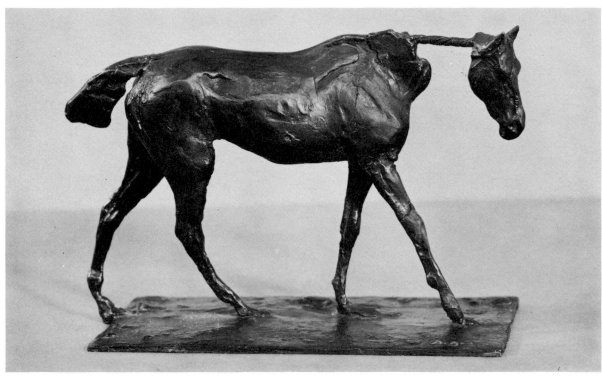

114. The Thoroughbred   Cire Perduc A.A. Hebrard $\frac{66}{A}$
Height: 5¼ inches R. V
Lent by The Metropolitan Museum of Art (The H. O. Havemeyer Collection)

115. Horse Galloping
     Height: 11⅞ inches R. VI
     Lent by The City Art Museum of St. Louis

116. Draught Horse   Cire Perdue A.A. Hebrard $\frac{30}{A}$
     Height: 4 inches R. VII
     Lent by The Metropolitan Museum of Art (The H. O. Havemeyer Collection)

117. Study of a Mustang   Cire Perdue A.A. Hebrard $\frac{21}{A}$
     Height: 8⅝ inches R. VIII
     Lent by The Metropolitan Museum of Art (The H. O. Havemeyer Collection)

118. Horse Clearing an Obstacle
     Height: 10½ inches R. IX
     *Lent by The Shelburne Museum (Mr. and Mrs. J. Watson Webb Collection)**

---

*Bronzes Nos. 118, 121, 122 and 124, lent by the Shelburne Museum, are permanently exhibited in the Electra Havemeyer Webb Memorial Building, which houses the art of the founders, Mr. and Mrs. J. Watson Webb.

119. Horse Walking   Cire Perdue A.A. Hebrard $\frac{10}{A}$

Height: 8¼ inches R. X

Lent by The Metropolitan Museum of Art (The H. O. Havemeyer Collection)

120. Horse Trotting   Cire Perdue A.A. Hebrard $\frac{49}{A}$

Height: 8⅝ inches R. XI

Lent by The Metropolitan Museum of Art (The H. O. Havemeyer Collection)

121. Rearing Horse
   Height: 12 inches R. XIII
   Lent by The Shelburne Museum
   (Mr. and Mrs. J. Watson Webb Collection)

122. Horse with Jockey Galloping
   Height: 9½ inches R. XIV-XV
   Lent by The Shelburne Museum (Mr. and Mrs. J. Watson Webb Collection)

123. Prancing Horse
    Height: 9⅜ inches R. XVI
    Lent Anonymously

124. Horse with Jockey Galloping
    Height: 11 inches R. XVII-XVIII
    Lent by The Shelburne Museum (Mr. and Mrs. J. Watson Webb Collection)

ADDENDA

EDGAR DEGAS
125. Riders on a Road, 1864-68
    Oil, 18½ x 23¾ inches   L. 121
    Lent by Mr. and Mrs. Nathan Cummings

JEAN BERAUD (1849-1936)
126. The Bookmakers at Longchamp
    Oil, 23½ x 15½ inches
    Lent by Mr. Edward Speelman

ISIDORE-JULES BONHEUR (1827-1901)
127. Jockey on a Horse
    Bronze, Height: 35 inches
    Lent by The Triangle Publications